Original title:
Foliage and Feelings

Copyright © 2025 Creative Arts Management OÜ
All rights reserved.

Author: Elliot Harrison
ISBN HARDBACK: 978-1-80581-808-3
ISBN PAPERBACK: 978-1-80581-335-4
ISBN EBOOK: 978-1-80581-808-3

Silence Fall's Whispering Heart

Leaves giggle as they twirl down,
Dancing like squirrels wearing crowns.
Branches play peek-a-boo with the sky,
While clouds huff and puff, oh my!

A pinecone plots to roll away,
Tickling grass in a cheeky play.
Acorns bounce, they laugh and cheer,
As if they know the end is near.

Rustling jokes in a breezy hum,
Nature's stand-up, full of fun.
Sunbeams tickle, shadows tease,
While autumn giggles with the breeze.

In this grove where chuckles bloom,
Every rustle chases gloom.
With each leaf's whisper, hearts do sway,
In laughter's arms, they frolic and play.

The Language of Rustling Leaves

In the garden, whispers play,
A dance of greens in bright array.
The wind chuckles through the trees,
As branches scratch their jokes, with ease.

Squirrels giggle up so high,
Chasing shadows in the sky.
A leaf trips over its own joke,
And lands in laughter, just like smoke.

Where Green Dreams Take Flight

In a patch of grass, dreams soar,
With butterflies who crave to explore.
The daisies wear their polka dots,
While ants parade with tiny pots.

A dandelion sings a tune,
While sunbeams join to make it swoon.
The petals giggle, it's no bluff,
As gnome hats dance, they've had enough!

Beneath the Boughs of Memory

Under branches, stories bloom,
Of kites tangled, bringing gloom.
A pinecone takes a boring seat,
While squirrels jest and can't be beat.

Old leaves chuckle, soft and sly,
Recalling times when clouds were shy.
They whisper of a prank gone wrong,
As sunlight hums a goofy song.

The Dance of Seasons and Souls

Each season spins with a silly flair,
As winter slips on a fresh pair.
Spring toes tap with a vibrant beat,
While summer bounces on its feet.

Autumn twirls in colorful capes,
And juggle-leaves hide silly shapes.
The earth chuckles loud and true,
In nature's waltz, we join the crew.

Shadows of a Whispered Canvas

Beneath the leafy shade we play,
Where laughter dances, come what may.
A squirrel steals snacks from my pack,
While trees exchange gossip from the back.

Colors chatter in the sun's embrace,
Making faces in this leafy space.
A palette spills secrets, oh so bright,
As shadows skip with sheer delight.

A gust of wind tickles my nose,
While petals giggle, oh how it goes!
The branches wave in a cheeky jest,
In this garden, we're all very blessed.

The Pulse of Life in Vibrant Shades

A cactus winks in the afternoon,
While daisies swing to a sunny tune.
The roses blush, they know a joke,
As bees buzz by, all cloaked in smoke.

Leaves flutter like a gossiping crowd,
Making the shy ones feel very proud.
In the forest's heart, mischief is rife,
With every branch, it shares its life.

A daffodil trips on a stray bee,
Creating laughter beneath the tree.
The colors clash in a playful fight,
Nature's own comedy, pure delight.

Sentiments Carried on Gentle Breezes

Whispers float on a breezy sigh,
While petals pirouette, oh me, oh my!
Grass tickles toes, whoops and yells,
As daisies play with hidden spells.

A leaf flutters down with a comical plop,
Landing on squirrels, who merely flop.
This leafy stage, a vibrant play,
Where all the greenery has something to say.

The sun peeks through leaves, a cheeky grin,
As nature's pranks make the good times spin.
With every rustle, a chuckle is near,
In this giggly glade, there's nothing to fear!

The Artistry of Nature's Touch

A paintbrush sways in the morning light,
As clouds giggle at the silly sight.
Flowers flaunt their brightest hues,
While butterflies wear mismatched shoes.

The ivy climbs with such bold flair,
It tickles trees with a gentle care.
In this wonderland, laughter blooms,
From playful sprouts to mischievous plumes.

Dandelions puff with a cheeky wink,
As they scatter dreams with a sudden blink.
Nature's canvas, a jester's delight,
Painting the world with colors so bright.

Melancholy Between the Branches

In the trees, a squirrel sighs,
Chasing nuts, he's full of lies.
"I'll store this one for winter's glee,"
Yet munches it right under a tree.

Beneath the leaves, a whisper grows,
A doe trips lightly, her grace opposed.
She giggles at the tangled vines,
Wishing for a shoe that shines.

A crow caws loud, but quite unwise,
Scaring folks who pass by with cries.
He's just here for the crumbly bread,
A jester, in a world of dread.

Branches shake with laughter light,
As nature gives a playful bite.
What's life without a little jest?
Amidst the leaves, we're all at rest.

A Walk Through Nature's Thoughts

On a path adorned with twirling leaves,
I wonder if the wind believes.
Does it tickle every blade just right?
Or laugh when trees get ticked off at night?

A hedgehog rolls like a furry ball,
In the midst of spring's grand hall.
With every bump, it sheds a grin,
Making the flowers laugh with kin.

Crickets chirp a rhythmic play,
While ants form a line, oh so gay.
They boast of treasures, oh what a deal!
Yet trip on their own feet—what a steal!

Beneath the sun, all seems quite swell,
Until a bee buzzes, ringing a bell.
Dancing flowers sway with delight,
Nature's show, a whimsical sight.

Leafy Layers of Untold Stories

A whisper from beneath the bark,
Claims a leaf is quite the lark.
"Listen here," it proudly beams,
"I've seen the world in my sunlit dreams."

Acorns argue, "I am the best,
A mighty oak shall stem from this nest!"
While the gossiping willows sway,
Saying, "Oh dear, let's not delay!"

A fox tiptoes, sporting style,
In borrowed leaves, oh what a guile!
With a flick of his bushy tail,
He giggles softly, telling a tale.

Each rustle tells a funny tease,
About the critters and their unease.
With every snap, a chuckle shared,
In leafy layers, laughter bared.

Embers of Warmth in Fall's Glow

Autumn drapes in threads of spice,
Pumpkin jokes don't come out nice.
A squirrel in shades of orange bright,
Thinks he's cool—oh, what a sight!

Leaves spiral down like confetti thrown,
As kids laugh, feeling right at home.
"Catch the falling, it's a rare prize!"
While one lands right in someone's eyes.

A chilly breeze brings in the fun,
But a cat jumps up and runs on the run.
With each leaf swish, there's giggly glee,
Ducks in a pond join in, carefree.

As bonfires crackle, stories unfold,
With ghostly gags, the bravest told.
In the warmth of glow, we find our cheer,
Laughter rises, drawing all near.

Swaying to the Rhythm of the Wind

In the park, a tree does dance,
Its branches twist in a silly prance.
Squirrels giggle, chasing about,
While leaves drop like confetti, no doubt.

A gust blows by, a hat takes flight,
Lands on a dog, what a funny sight!
The flowers laugh with colors so bright,
Nature's joke turns day into night.

Breezes whisper, tickling the air,
Dancing twigs make jokes without a care.
A frisky breeze plays hide and seek,
While giggles flow, soft and cheek to cheek.

With each gust, a comic relief,
Nature's stage, a joyful belief.
Trees act out, caught in the show,
Laughter flows where green things grow.

Echoes in the Thicket

In the bushes, whispers rise,
A bird mocks, what a great disguise!
Rabbits hop, having their fun,
While shadows play, hiding from the sun.

A leaf falls down, gets stuck in a bush,
Nature's prank, sudden as a rush.
The crickets chirp a tune so odd,
Celebrating life, giving a nod.

Branches creak like an old man's cough,
While the wind giggles, telling us off.
The backdrop of laughter, rustle, and cheer,
Tells tales of nature, far and near.

From the thicket, echoes rebound,
In this leafy theater, joy is found.
With every sound, a chuckle or two,
Life in the woods has much to do.

The Language of Rustling Leaves

Leaves chatter in a playful spree,
Sharing secrets of a busy tree.
Whispers twist, turn to a joke,
As acorns tumble, and the branches poke.

A breeze interrupts, with a flair so bold,
Tickling the bark, teasing the old.
The sun winks down, bright and sly,
Curious insects buzz nearby.

Trees lay gossip as seasons flow,
Tall tales told in a gentle show.
Mischievous shadows dance in delight,
While nature chuckles, day turns to night.

With every rustle, a jest unfolds,
In laughter's embrace, the green world holds.
The wind recites, and colors reply,
In this merry circle, we all fly high.

Fragments of a Sunlit Path

Sunbeams dance, casting playful dots,
While petals laugh in secret spots.
A path unfolds, with quirks and turns,
Each step reveals what the daylight earns.

Critters scuttle, their antics grand,
Chasing shadows, a wild band.
A squirrel sneezes, leaves flutter around,
Nature's laugh is a joyful sound.

With each stumble, the flowers cheer,
Bouncing with joy as I draw near.
Spilling laughter along the way,
Sunlit paths invite us to play.

Underneath the golden hue,
The earth chuckles, with mischief too.
Joy bursts forth, and woes are cast,
In the sunlit moments, every laugh lasts.

Secrets in the Shade

Under a leaf, I hide my snack,
A squirrel smiles, picking up the slack.
Why do trees always seem to jest?
Their laughter echoes, a funny quest.

In the shadows, whispers bloom,
As squirrels dance, dispelling gloom.
A deer croaks jokes, suddenly absurd,
While branches giggle, as if they've heard.

Rustled leaves tickle my nose,
Fickle breezes, where mischief grows.
Nature's comedy, a playful scene,
With punchlines hidden where grass is green.

In the cool nook, secrets unfold,
Jokes of pine cones, both brave and bold.
I stifle laughter, oh what a shame,
That even trees can play the game.

Heartbeats Amongst Hazel Branches

Beneath the canopy, I hear a tune,
A chipmunk croons beneath the moon.
Two bunnies argue, who eats the most?
While hazel branches play the host.

Tickling leaves begin to sway,
As squirrels dance cheeky ballet.
Branches overhead wink and nod,
While acorns giggle, oh so odd.

Frisky foliage boasts its clout,
With breezy jokes, there's never doubt.
A bush spins tales of a feathered feat,
As laughter swells across the street.

In the leafy arms of nature's fun,
Heartbeats mingle, twain become one.
Who knew that trees could tell such tales?
With giggles trapped in wind-eroded gales.

The Palette of a Daydream

Colors mingle where shadows sway,
With hues of humor come out to play.
Leaves wear giggles, a whimsical cloak,
As blossoms burst forth with a chuckle or poke.

Within the brush of green and gold,
A rabbit loiters, feeling bold.
He tells a yarn of colors grand,
While violets roll across the land.

Sunlight splatters a canvas bright,
A symphony of laughter, pure delight.
Crisp carrot tops share silly jokes,
As butterflies flutter and spin, like folks.

In daydream's slipstream, jesters abound,
With nature's palette, joy is found.
Laughter flows like paint in streams,
Savoring warmth in colorful dreams.

Breezes that Whisper Love

In the garden where petals play,
Breezes giggle, what do they say?
"Shh, listen close," the daisies grin,
As whispers swirl and begin to spin.

A breeze tickles, with secrets shared,
As leaves chuckle, feeling prepared.
"Who knew love was such a tease?"
The bushes murmur, swaying with ease.

Twisted vines exchange some glee,
As sunlight dances, carefree spree.
Every flutter and rustle sings,
Of silly tales, oh, what joy it brings.

With every gust a new joke's born,
In the blush of dawn, a day reborn.
So we heed the whispers, let laughter ring,
In the breeze, where love finds its wings.

The Colors of a Heart Unfurled

In the garden of laughter, bright hues do play,
Painted petals gossip about love's silly way.
A crimson joke tickles a shy shade of green,
While yellow dandelions puff at the scene.

Blushing blooms giggle, twisting in the breeze,
Each frolicsome flower shares secrets with bees.
A purple punchline lands, soft giggles arise,
As the sun beams a grin towards bright spinning skies.

Dancing Shadows of Pine

Under tall sentinels with bark like old jokes,
A waltz of the shadows, where humor invokes.
Swaying to whispers that tickle the air,
Those tall, ticking trees tell tall tales with flair.

The needles are giggling, a mischievous bunch,
They tickle the squirrels, who pause for their lunch.
As laughter erupts from a breeze full of sass,
Each shadowy shimmer matches the class.

Funky fungi prance in their spore-laden boots,
While fun-loving ferns give a nod to the roots.

Petals and Pondering

Little buds mull over the sun's bright cheek,
While petals exchange tales, oh so unique.
A daisy debates with a dandelion's wish,
On the meaning of beauty in a flowery dish.

A stem in the sunlight stretches and sighs,
As petals quip about the passing flies.
Oh, the ponderous lightness that humor can brew,
As blooms share a chuckle on morning's bright hue.

In the cauldron of colors, absurdity brews,
With goofy green grass proposing wild views.

Green Dreams in a Parched World

Under a sun that laughs at the cracked earth below,
Emerald wishes sprout, putting on quite a show.
Cactus and clover, both cracking up wide,
Trading wise jokes 'bout the drought they abide.

With each droplet cherished, like stories retold,
The smallest of greens shares a wink, oh so bold.
A thistle in jest lifts a tiny green fist,
While weeds wrap around dreams that nobody missed.

When rain brings a chuckle, it's quite the affair,
As leaves toast the skies with a jubilant flair.

Stemmed Hues of Longing

In the garden of hopes, I found a sprout,
With dreams so tall, they forgot about.
A daisy tried to flirt with a weed,
While the chubby bumblebee missed his feed.

Twirling leaves whispered secrets unheard,
While the grass tried to dance, but it just blurred.
A daffodil giggled, bright and proud,
As the shy fern waved from beneath the cloud.

The tulips dressed up, oh so bright,
Causing all the dandelions to take flight.
But one fell down in a hapless croquet,
Yelling, "Next time, I'll stick to my bouquet!"

Still, the garden dreams in color so bold,
With petals that laugh, their stories told.
As I wander through joy, a heart so light,
I chase after laughs as they take to flight.

Blush of Life's Transience

The sunset paints the sky in blush,
While squirrels make a napping hush.
Leaves flutter-down like giggles on air,
Tickling the ground without a care.

A hawk swoops down for a snack or two,
While a rabbit twitches, unsure what to do.
The pumpkin grins in its vibrant coat,
Thinking, 'Oh my, I'm ready to float!'

With shadows long, and whispers sly,
The crickets start a band nearby.
Frogs in the pond croak hit tunes with flair,
As dancing leaves perform without a care.

In this fleeting realm where laughter grows,
Nature chuckles in its leafy prose.
The illusion of time, a playful tease,
As blades of grass sway in the gentle breeze.

Boughs that Bend and Surrender

The branches bend with a comical style,
Bow low to the ground, then boast like a child.
A woodpecker taps out a secret code,
While acorns giggle, sharing the load.

The wind tells jokes in a rustling tone,
As bark pretends to be a stepping stone.
Leaves hold their breath for the next big breeze,
Ready to tumble with the greatest of ease.

A squirrel skitters, with treasures to hoard,
While wise old owls feel quite adored.
But the raccoons laugh, plundering by night,
Claiming, "We're artists! Who needs daylight?"

In this dance of time, the trees take a chance,
Waving to life in a whimsical dance.
Surrender, they say, to the joyful flight,
As nature chuckles beneath the moonlight.

Heartbeats in Hollowed Tree Trunks

Inside a tree trunk, whispers of cheer,
Creatures convene, no hint of fear.
With ants in tuxedos, ready to prance,
While beetles compete for a chance to enhance.

A woodpecker's showy, a tap and a sway,
Tickling the bark, "Hey, you wanna play?"
Every echo reveals stories old,
As the saplings giggle, bold and unrolled.

But oh, the raccoons with masks on their face,
Steal the spotlight in this leafy space.
Mice in their bonnets twirl to and fro,
Forgetting the time as friendships grow.

So let's gather 'round in this trunk so fair,
With laughter and joy swaying in the air.
The heartbeat of nature, a rhythm so sweet,
As stories unfold beneath nimble feet.

Beneath the Boughs of Yesterday

The trees gossiped loud, what a sight,
Leaves dancing with giggles, what a light.
Squirrels snickered, scampered with glee,
Dropping acorns like jokes from a spree.

Sunlight peeked through with a playful grin,
Tickling the branches, coaxing them in.
A breeze made a joke, rustling the leaves,
"Why don't you come down? Just roll up your sleeves!"

Roots tangled in laughter, their jokes never old,
Each twist and turn, a story retold.
The shade chuckled softly, holding a grin,
Whispering secrets that spark joy within.

Beneath these boughs, life's lighter and bright,
With every chuckle, the world feels just right.
Nature's own humor, with warmth to impart,
A joyful reminder, it tickles the heart.

The Touch of Earth's Breath

The whisper of dirt said, "Take a deep whiff!"
A dandelion waved, a playful gift.
"Blow me away!" it yelled with a cheer,
And off flew the seeds, like jokes in the air.

The sunlight sneezed, what a ruckus it made,
While shadows just giggled, happily played.
Each pebble chuckled, no worry in sight,
"We're just rock stars, basking in daylight!"

The flowers all danced, giving off cheer,
With petals like confetti, "Join us, my dear!"
The worms held a party, a wiggle and twist,
In the garden of laughter, no chance to be missed.

The earth's breath is silly, it tickles the ground,
With laughter erupting in soft, mellow sounds.
When we stop and listen, life's quirks we will find,
In nature's own humor, happiness is blind.

Veins of Nature's Canvas

A branch painted jokes in hues so bright,
With colors that play under sunlight.
"What happened to leaves that got lost on their way?"
They answer with rustles, "We just like to play!"

A painter with nature, so vibrant and free,
Splashed colors of laughter on each bending tree.
Dancing in sync with a laugh and a twist,
Creating a masterpiece that no one could resist.

The clouds joined in, daring to play,
"Let's cuddle in laughter, just lying this way!"
Each tree held a grin, roots deep in delight,
With whispers of wind that made everything light.

And so nature's canvas, imperfectly funny,
Is filled with the warmth of a day sunny.
In the pulse of the green, a rhythm that's grand,
A harmony blooming, playful, unplanned.

Crimson Secrets in Twilight

As evening approached, the trees did confer,
With red leaves all whispering, "What's your prefer?"
"Being sky-high or resting below?"
They chuckled together, quite a lively show.

The moon peeked in, adjusting its tie,
Said, "Don't mind me, I'm just passing by."
A nocturnal critter held up a sign,
"Laughing is crucial, let's all intertwine!"

The shadows unfurled, with stories to lend,
While colors of sunset began to blend.
Each twinkling star joined in the brawl,
"Shooting stars are real, let's have a ball!"

Crimson secrets whispered, floating in air,
Holding hands with laughter, without a care.
As night wrapped around with a joyous embrace,
Nature's own laughter brightened the space.

Under the Arched Canopy

Beneath the wide expanse, we twirl,
Leaves like confetti, a leafy swirl.
Squirrels overheard plotting their schemes,
While we laugh at their nutty dreams.

A branch swings low, a hat knocked askew,
A bird chirps loud, giving titters too.
We dodge the drops, from skies that drip,
With umbrellas of greenery, we take a trip.

The ground is a carpet, squishy and fun,
With muddied shoes, we've only just begun.
Laughter echoes, as we stumble about,
In our forest parade, it's impossible to pout.

So let the branches weave tales up high,
While we dance below, with a jubilant sigh.
Here in the woods, all worries depart,
With every good chuckle, we lighten the heart.

Ivory Moonlight on Leafy Canopies

Under the moon, in a silver glow,
Trees play hide and seek, just for show.
With shadows that jiggle, and branches that jive,
The night comes alive, oh what a hive!

We stumble on roots, trip over brambles,
Splitting our sides at our awkward gambles.
A raccoon peers out, wearing a grin,
It seems even critters love a good spin.

The air's thick with giggles, some whispers too,
As we dance like dandelions, entirely askew.
With the light shining down, like a spotlight's beam,
We're the stars of this night, living our dream.

So let's sway with the breeze, let our worries go,
Here beneath the stars, everything's a show.
In this nightly theater, we act our part,
With laughter as the script, and joy in our heart.

The Aroma of Whispering Pines

Between the tall trunks, secrets do glide,
While we chase after scents that the breezes provide.
Pinecones tumble down, landing near feet,
As we chuckle at nature's peculiar treat.

The whispers of branches, a giggling gale,
Telling us stories of epic detail.
Each rustling leaf makes us burst out in glee,
Like nature's own soundtrack, a jubilant spree.

With hats made of leaves and sticks in our hands,
We're warriors of laughter, defending our lands.
The tang of fresh pine, it fills up the air,
Turns our wild antics into a grand affair.

So let's climb the hills, let our spirits soar,
Through this whimsical grove, we just want more.
With each step a joke, and each glance a grin,
We weave through the pines, letting fun times begin.

Nostalgic Trails Paved in Green

On paths lined with memories, laughter in store,
We dodge the tall nettles, giggling galore.
Old sneakers squish on the soft, damp ground,
In every muddy puddle, joy can be found.

The trees share their tales, sounding quite funny,
As we reminisce days that were bright and sunny.
Each twig that snaps holds a memory dear,
Bringing back moments of laughter and cheer.

Scurrying squirrels join in the fun,
Darting from shadows, they race and run.
With giggles and glee, we roam far and wide,
In our kingdom of green, where we'll always reside.

So let us embrace all this whimsy today,
With nature as stage, come out and play.
For each step we take, in this paradise green,
We create endless laughter, a blissful scene.

Rustling Echoes of Solitude

A crisp crunch beneath my shoe,
Squirrels laugh at my debut.
Leaves gossip in the gentle chill,
Nature's drama, quite the thrill.

Branches sway, in jest they tease,
Whispers carried by the breeze.
I step lightly, but hear the shout,
'Adventurer!' they laugh about.

The shadows roll in shiny coats,
As I trip over rogue toads.
Nature mocks with every squeak,
In this comedy, I'm the freak.

Sun dips low, a playful wink,
Leaves dance, and I can't think.
Joke's on me, I can't resist,
This quirky world, too good to miss.

Twilight's Embrace in Leafy Arms

At dusk, the shadows stretch so wide,
A leafy curtain, the sun won't hide.
I waddle through with a careless grin,
Pretending to be a berry's kin.

The wind giggles, oh what a tease,
It plays tag with the vibrant trees.
One leaf flutters right past my ear,
'Take that!' it whispers, loud and clear.

Crickets tune in to make me laugh,
Their chirps draw maps of a silly path.
I stumble through this twilight maze,
Caught in nature's unending gaze.

As night wraps up, I jive with stars,
Leaves join in from afar.
In this gloaming, the echoes cheer,
It's a hilarious parade, loud and clear!

The Throughline of the Breeze

A gust flits past, what a surprise,
It tickles my nose, oh how time flies.
The trees chorus with rustling rhymes,
Catching me off guard in these times.

I chase the wind - it's such a tease,
It twirls away like a sloppy breeze.
Through branches wild and tangled laughs,
I imagine it's pulling my shafts.

Each leaf's a jester in this grand play,
Mimicking dancers in disarray.
I join their ranks, with a silly fling,
In the throes of wind, oh how we swing!

I tilt my hat to the blowing spree,
Swaying and spinning, just like a bee.
Who knew this air could spark delight?
In this caper, I found my flight.

Gesture of the Withering Green

The last leaf clings, oh let it stay,
With dramatic flair, it shouts 'Hooray!'
While others twirl down without a care,
This green diva won't go anywhere.

A breeze blows in and gives a nudge,
'Come on now, it's time to budge!'
It rolls its eyes, then takes a bow,
The drama's thick, as time allows.

Grounded leaves chuckle, a riotous scene,
While I slip on what's lost, quite obscene.
Nature's comedy never ends,
Laughter sprouts like mischievous friends.

So here I fall, in mirth I'm caught,
Where leafy debauchery's always sought.
As evening whispers sweet farewells,
Join this circus where joy compels.

Wandering Through a Labyrinth of Light

In a maze of greens and browns,
Where shadows dance, and giggles drown.
I trip on roots, they laugh and tease,
As sunlight plays with playful breeze.

A squirrel points, with tiny paws,
At glowing maps, he's got no flaws.
I stumble forth on a wild quest,
Chasing giggles, I must be blessed.

Each turn reveals a shocking sight,
A flower tickles, oh what a fright!
I swear it winked, now that's a twist,
Nature's jesters on my list.

With every step, a prank unfolds,
The forest shines with stories bold.
I laugh so hard, the trees do sway,
Join the fun, here we'll all play.

Reflections in Leafy Mirrors

In puddles bright, the leaves do flop,
I see my face, a silly pop!
A dorky grin with muddy glee,
The trees are snickering at me!

There's a twig that whispers, 'Hey, look here!'
I wink back at it, full of cheer.
The branches wave, just like a crowd,
My laughter bursts, obnoxious, loud.

The sunlight glimmers off each face,
Branches dance in a wild race.
I mimic them, all limbs akimbo,
Nature hosting its own disco.

A bird drops a joke, I nearly fall,
This wooded stage, it has it all.
In reflective pools, I see it shine,
A comedy formed in nature's design.

Colors that Whisper 'Home'

A cloak of colors wraps me tight,
In reds and golds, oh what a sight!
The ground is crunching, laughter grows,
As autumn flaunts its fancy clothes.

The painted leaves are cheeky fools,
They swirl around like playful schools.
I try to catch them, what a game,
But they just dance, and I feel lame.

A vibrant hue taps on my shoe,
It giggles softly, 'Come play too!'
With every step, they cheer and spin,
I find my heart's own silly grin.

As sunset glows, the colors hum,
A symphony of fun, oh what a drum!
These lively shades, like friends of old,
Whisper tales of warmth, bright and bold.

The Hidden Heart of the Forest

In the secret nooks, where giggles hide,
A mushroom bounces, oh what a ride!
With every giggle, the underbrush shakes,
The forest harbors all of our pranks.

Beneath the boughs, whispers collide,
A tree trunk dances, what a wild stride!
I join the waltz, in my finest shoes,
Sticking my tongue out to the woods' views.

A mischievous breeze tugs at my coat,
It spins me around like a playful boat.
The squirrels cheer from the branches above,
This wild heart beats with humor and love.

As dusk unfurls its twilight blend,
The forest jokes, they never end.
In nature's laugh, I find my place,
In the heart of mischief, I embrace the space.

Treetops Holding Secrets of Solace

In the treetops, critters plot,
Squirrel in shades, a jester's lot.
Chasing leaves like playful ghosts,
What they seek? Well, no one knows.

Branches bend with laughter's tune,
Breezes dance beneath the moon.
Whispers of a sneaky breeze,
Tickle trees, bring them to tease.

Glimmering tricks in shadows high,
Leaves wear masks, oh me, oh my!
Pinecones scheming, just for fun,
Hidden hijinks 'til day is done.

Watching clouds and making bets,
Nature's laughs are the safest sets.
Join the show, don't take a snooze,
Life's a play, don't miss your cues!

Sighs of Forgotten Woods

In quiet groves where mischief sleeps,
Tree trunks gossip, secrets they keep.
Mossy carpets hide things of yore,
Fungi giggle, what's behind that door?

Branches wave like a quirky crew,
Whispering tales of me and you.
Spot the raccoon with his grand escape,
Master of crafts, with a puzzling shape.

Squirrels roll acorns down the hill,
Like tiny bombs, what a thrill!
Leaves chuckle as they tumble down,
Nature's humor, a frolic crown.

The woods wear smiles beneath the boughs,
Laughing with shadows, taking their vows.
With every rustle, old jokes awake,
Binding the woods where silliness makes!

The Tangle of Roots and Dreams

Beneath the surface, roots entwine,
Whispers shared over some cheap wine.
Mice on a quest, a cheese-filled scheme,
Gathering gossip, living the dream.

Tangles of dreams like a busy net,
Chasing lost thoughts, oh what a fret!
Strange mushrooms rise to tell their tales,
Winking at passing, nonchalant snails.

Curly vines dance in a silly style,
Twisting and turning, oh what a while.
Each knot a story, a giggle, a tease,
Tickling roots as they dangle with ease.

Explore the depths with a chuckle or two,
Nature's mishaps, surprises anew.
In the tangle, find laughter's beam,
Beneath the earth, there's a crazy dream!

Horizon of Flickering Shadows

At dusk when shadows start to sway,
Laughter flickers in a playful way.
Join the fireflies in their frantic flight,
Dancing like sprites in the fading light.

Tall grasses whisper of silly sins,
Tales of the day where mischief wins.
Bumblebees buzz with a comedic zing,
Chasing their tails in a hapless fling.

Crickets chirp with a rhythmic jest,
Their nightly tune, a funny fest.
In the fading glow, the world seems bright,
Every flicker holds pure delight.

As stars wink down in their cosmic play,
The night wears a grin, come what may.
So raise a toast to the quirks we own,
In shadows and laughter, we find our home!

The Stillness in the Midst of Change.

In a breeze, they dance and swirl,
Mischief on each leaf's unfurl.
Sometimes they tickle passing noses,
Nature's laughter, like a rose's.

Underfoot, a crunchy bed,
As squirrels plot their nutty spread.
Funny how they spin and prance,
While we just waddle in a trance.

Branches sway, a secret show,
Whispering tales to passersby, slow.
Oh, to be a leaf up high,
Trading gossip as clouds drift by.

As moments flutter, it's not all grim,
For every branch has its own whim.
Maybe next time, I'll join the spree,
And let the wind carry me with glee!

Whispers of Autumn's Embrace

Golden hues with a cheeky smile,
Every step, a crunchy aisle.
Who knew colors could be so bright?
Nature's jest in the fading light.

Pumpkin spice and rolling leaves,
Squirrels dance as if on eaves.
They stash away their prized finds,
While we just laugh, lost in minds.

A breeze brings chuckles from afar,
Nature's quirks, a shining star.
In each gust, a playful wink,
Leaves giggle, "Come on, don't just think!"

With every rustle, secrets spill,
Tales of gusts that give a thrill.
Let's join in this leafy cheer,
Autumn's jokes, we hold most dear.

Beneath the Canopy of Memory

Underneath this vibrant shade,
Where shadows play, and light is made.
You might find a wandering gnome,
Thinking this place is his home.

Old benches creak with laughter, too,
As birds chirp tunes that feel so true.
Leaves whisper tales of days gone past,
While we giggle, making moments last.

Branches stretch like curious hands,
Pointing out the fun-filled lands.
What secrets do the roots conceal?
Oh, the stories they could reveal!

In this world where time's a friend,
Memories twist and never end.
So grab a leaf, give it a toss,
And let your worries take a loss.

Leaves that Hold Secrets

A rustling leaf knows your name,
In its presence, we're all the same.
What mischief hides in each green fold?
Nature's stories waiting to be told.

Oh, the tales of drizzle and sun,
How clouds played as they had their fun.
Each leaf dances, every twist,
Mimicking moments you might have missed.

In shades of laughter, they unfold,
Whispering dreams, both shy and bold.
What's that? A spark? A flying wish?
Caught up in wonder, you can't dismiss.

As twilight wraps in a leafy hug,
Every crackle gives a tug.
Let's gather 'round these whispers sweet,
And dance along to nature's beat.

Songs of Unseen Roots

In the garden, a chicken crows,
Telling tales that only she knows,
Dance with worms, they wiggle in glee,
While radishes laugh beneath the tea.

Squirrels plan world domination,
As they plot from their lofty station,
The onions cry, "not again, oh dear!"
While beans smile, hiding their fear.

Petunias gossip behind the shed,
Comparing hats made of baked bread,
Sunflowers twist in a humorous beat,
While dandelions toast to their feat.

Lettuce giggles, then splatters around,
As raindrops dance on the squishy ground,
A cabbage sings in a raspy voice,
In this veggie patch, we all rejoice!

The Soft Touch of Nature's Pulse

Watermelons mime a summer show,
While cherries giggle in bright row,
The breeze whispers secrets with a laugh,
As cucumbers try to take a photograph.

Roses wear their prickly crown,
While the daisies gossip about the town,
Bumblebees buzzing, casting spells,
Chasing shadows where mischief dwells.

Clouds play hide and seek in the sun,
With shadows prancing, oh what fun!
Lilies sip tea with a royal flair,
As ants debate if life's truly fair.

Sprouts in a dance-off, twirl with pride,
While broccoli watches, eyes open wide,
In this lively grove, you can hear the cheer,
Of laughter blossoming far and near!

The Journey of a Wandering Breeze

A breeze whirls past, throwing hats in the air,
Grabbing the lawn chairs – oh, what a scare!
Kites giggle overhead like silly old fools,
While wobbly blossoms twist into pools.

Clouds toss popcorn over grassy lands,
The sun plays catch with the silly hands,
Frogs jump high, attempting to sing,
As dragonflies dance on a gossamer string.

Trees swap stories with the rustling leaves,
While raccoons shuffle like naughty thieves,
A playful gust tickles the springtime scene,
Where laughter blooms and the grass grows green.

A flower sneezes, proclaiming a fact,
That plants have feelings, it's quite an act!
As shadows join in this whimsical spree,
The world chuckles softly, as if to agree.

Tints of Heart's Ambiguity

A daisy dreams of a rose-red heart,
While marigolds practice their art,
The wind sways, mismatching pairs,
With ferns in tutus, and wild stares.

Buds compete in a comedy show,
While spritzing water makes eyebrows grow,
A sunflower frets, seeking applause,
While worms audition for dandelion flaws.

Mixing colors like a painter's dish,
Where violets plot a mischievous wish,
Blades of grass gossip, oh so sly,
As hedgehogs snicker and waddle by.

In this patch of jests, all's fair and bright,
Where every bloom adds a splash of light,
A chorus of giggles fills the cool space,
With whispers of humor in nature's embrace!

Murmurs of the Woodland Heart

In the forest where squirrels conspire,
Gossip flows like a bubbling brook's choir.
Leaves chuckle softly in the warm breeze,
While raccoons play poker beneath the trees.

Acorns drop with a thud, oh dear,
As the wise old owl just rolls an eye here.
Branches sway with a whimsical dance,
Making mushrooms giggle, giving fungi a chance.

A fox tells tales of night-time snacks,
While the porcupine teases the unknowing packs.
The deer join in with a scampering beat,
As they prance and twirl on their nimble feet.

Under the moon, the laughter grows loud,
Each tree a member of this leafy crowd.
With a rustle and shake, the night turns absurd,
In a world where silence is utterly unheard.

Shadows Stretching Beneath the Sunset

In the twilight's glow, shadows begin to play,
Stretching and yawning, they dance the day away.
A shadowy cat pranks a wise old fox,
Who stumbles back, in a tangle of socks!

The sun dips low, painting the sky,
Clouds in silly hats start to drift by.
A giggle erupts from a corner of red,
As the grass whispers secrets, none will be said.

Branches twist, trying to reach the stars,
While critters on scooters zoom past in cars!
A hedgehog declares he's the king of the fun,
While ants hold a concert, in unison sung.

In this glowing hour, laughter ignites,
As the sun winks, bidding farewell to the sights.
With chuckles and glee the daylight departs,
Leaving shadows to cradle the light in their hearts.

The Heart's Echo in Maple's Shade

Beneath sweet branches, secrets unfold,
Maple whispers softly, so bold.
Its leaves wear colors, like clowns at a fair,
Tickling the wind with a jester's flair.

Squirrels play tag, in a friendly race,
While chipmunks argue about their space.
A laughter erupts from a nearby glade,
As the breeze tells a joke that simply won't fade.

With a rustle here, and a rustle there,
A hedgehog contemplates, sighing in despair.
"Why can't I fly like that bird up high?"
But the maple just chuckles and gives him a sigh.

So under this tree, the hilarity flows,
Each critter a friend, where silliness grows.
With echoes of laughter, we gather our cheer,
In the glorious shade, where we cast off our fear.

Canopies of Unspoken Words

Up above, the branches weave a chat,
Murmurs burst forth from a nearby cat.
It sprawls on a branch, feeling so wise,
While listening close to the whispers of skies.

With rustling leaves forming funny remarks,
And cawing crows taking note of the larks.
A jester-like rabbit hops through the aisle,
Making the very trees laugh with his style.

Under the canopy, the sun starts to pout,
Feeling left out, as the shadows just shout.
"Join us!" they plead, "We're a funny old crew,
In this wild tapestry, there's always room for you!"

So the sun beams down with a playful grin,
As laughter expands where the wild things begin.
In this lovely arch where no one feels shy,
Let's spin our wild tales, where giggles can fly.

Treetops and Tranquility

In the treetops where squirrels dare,
Chasing shadows without a care.
They plot and scheme, a nutty affair,
While birds gossip, unaware.

Leaves rustle with laughter's sound,
As branches bend, a playful bound.
One leaf slips and tumbles down,
A whimsical dance, all around.

The sun peeks through in a silly grin,
Tickling trunks, letting light in.
Nature's own comedy, where I begin,
Joined by a chorus of chirps and din.

So up in the boughs, let worry cease,
In this green theatre, find your peace.
Join nature's folly, let your heart lease,
Embrace the humor—laugh, release.

Reflections in the Dewy Dawn

Morning dew on blades of green,
Whispers secrets, crisp and keen.
Each drop's a giggle, neat and clean,
Nature's jewels, shy and serene.

Sunrise chuckles, paints the sky,
While sleepy critters rub an eye.
A rabbit trips, oh my, oh my!
Jumping haphazardly, asking why.

Breezes tease the flowers' heads,
Among the petals, playful spreads.
A bee buzzes, wearing hats of reds,
In this awakening, joy embeds.

Dewy dawn, with laughter's tone,
Unruly moments, widely known.
Nature's jesters put on a show,
Reflections spark, and joy will grow.

The Silence of a Leaf Unturned

A lone leaf hangs, silent and still,
Pondering life, yet needing a thrill.
It's rather boring, this situation,
So it dreams up wild concoctions.

Conversations with the breezy air,
As it sways with a devil-may-care.
Beneath, a critter starts his scare,
Shouting, "Hello! You're quite a rare!"

Moments pass like echoes of laughter,
Does a leaf ponder what comes after?
A wish to twirl, to flap and to flutter,
Yet stuck in contemplation—oh, what a clutter!

But when it turns, oh what a sight,
A flap, a whirl, pure delight!
In the wind's embrace, it finds its might,
The silence broken, laughter takes flight.

Mosaic of Nostalgia

Colors splatter, oh what a scene,
Painting memories, bright and keen.
Dancing shadows on the green,
A mosaic thread, very serene.

Fallen leaves, like tales untold,
Each crisp crackle a memory bold.
Whispers of summers, young and old,
In every hue, a piece of gold.

Squirrels scamper, mischief in mind,
Collecting treasures they sometimes find.
While the sun giggles, forever kind,
Warming the heart that's intertwined.

So stitch the past with present cheer,
In nature's quilt, hold what is dear.
A tapestry woven, year by year,
In laughter's embrace, we persevere.

Whispers of Autumn's Embrace

The leaves they dance, a silly show,
Swinging with laughter, to and fro.
They tickle the breeze, with swirls and spins,
Each gust a giggle, where joy begins.

Crimson and gold in a messy pile,
A jump sends them flying with childlike guile.
Splat! On the ground! Oh what a sight!
Who knew the trees could party all night?

Chasing the wind, rustling in glee,
Squirrels join in, as loud as can be.
Chattering loudly, dashing about,
"Hey, pass the acorn!" they scream and shout.

When branches bow low, you can hear them tease,
"Catch me if you can, oh do, if you please!"
The humor of nature, alive with delight,
An autumnal wonder, a whimsical night.

Beneath the Canopy of Hearts

Under the trees where shadows play,
Sunbeams peek out, in a cheeky way.
A branch overhead, swings down with a rush,
And lands on my hat—oh what a hush!

Giggles erupt from the bushes nearby,
As critters plot stunts, oh my, oh my!
They slapstick around, a slap on the back,
But tumble and roll, oh where's the knack?

A couple of leaves, sneaky and smug,
Hide in the grass, giving shy bugs a hug.
"Let's prank the whole world!" they whisper and grin,
And the sun shines brighter, the mischief to begin.

Laughter rises, like sap from the trees,
In this gentle ballet, all dance as they please.
With every flutter, and every prance,
Nature has come out for a joyous dance!

A Tapestry of Colors

A splash of red, and a dash of gold,
The palette of nature, brave and bold.
Leaves shake and shimmer, in a fluttering spree,
Winking at passers, "Come join our jamboree!"

Amidst the hues, a parrot appears,
Mocking the whispers, the giggles, the cheers.
"Who ordered this mess of confetti on ground?
I might just take part, oh what have I found?"

A giddy old oak, with branches askew,
Cracks jokes with the birch, "I can't see you!"
The maple chimes in, "You look a bit bright!
Time for a dip, let's party tonight!"

As dusk settles in, a blanket so warm,
The trees keep on chuckling, clearly no harm.
In this world of color, a carnival spree,
Joy can be found from the roots to the leaves!

Secrets Held in Leafy Shadows

In corners of groves, secrets do dwell,
Where giggles and whispers weave their own spell.
As leaves brush the ground, a tattle-tale breeze,
Spreads stories of squirrels with acorned keys.

Oh watch out, my friend, for the sneaky fawn,
Dashing and darting, come the early dawn.
With a wink and a scamper, it plays hide and seek,
While the shadows chuckle, in games so unique.

A mystery lies in the rustling sound,
Where laughter is buried, and joy can be found.
Each rattle of branches unveils a jest,
Nature's own riddle, at its very best.

As twilight descends, in this leafy abode,
The secrets keep swirling, untying the load.
With shadows and laughter, they twirl in delight,
While the world outside sighs, saying goodnight.

A Tapestry of Seasons' Sighs

The leaves wear colors, a comic show,
Red, yellow, and green, they steal the glow.
Squirrels in top hats, with acorns to toss,
They dance in circles, thinking they're the boss.

Autumn's jokes land with a crisp little snap,
Nature's punchlines in a leafy wrap.
Breezes giggle as they tickle the trees,
Whispers of laughter ride along with the breeze.

Then winter arrives, cold jokes on the sly,
Snowflakes tumble, all aiming to fly.
They land on the ground, a twist and a freeze,
Making the world look like a soft, frosty tease.

Spring bursts forth, all laughter and cheer,
Flowers bloom bright, they simply won't fear.
Daisies chuckle as bunnies hop by,
In a world that's grinning, beneath a blue sky.

Beneath the Orchard's Gaze

An orchard of giggles, apples aglow,
Dance with delight, in a jovial row.
Bees buzz melodies, so sweet and absurd,
Even the worms hum a whimsical word!

Branches hold secrets, of laughter up high,
A chuckle with cherries, and a wink from the pie.
Grapes whisper jokes, in clusters they share,
With every pluck, they burst forth with flair.

Sunset arrives, in a shimmer of gold,
The fruits trade jests, some daring, some bold.
Under the stars, ripe jokes fill the air,
The orchard is alive, with humor to spare.

Morning breaks cautious, but soon it will play,
The laughter of cicadas joins in the fray.
Each day a riot, beneath boughs so wide,
Where humor spills forth, like a joyous tide.

When Petals Fall into Quietude

Petals pirouette, with a fluttering flair,
Twirling down gently, a soft, fragrant air.
Nature's confetti, tossed from above,
A dance for the careless, a jest from the love.

They gather in piles, so bright and alive,
Each landing a giggle, they wiggle and jive.
Ants march in silence, while bees chuckle loud,
At this leafy fun fest, in their bustling crowd.

The breeze pulls a prank, wraps them tight in a swirl,
Leaves tickle each petal, in a whimsical whirl.
As twilight descends, they nestle in sleep,
Dreaming of laughter, concealed in a heap.

Dawn brings a chuckle, as one petal peeks,
A wink to the sunlight, its humor it seeks.
The cycle continues, in nature's great play,
Where jokes fall like petals, brightening the day.

The Lullaby of Lasting Green

In a world painted green, a fun little sight,
Crickets serenade as day turns to night.
The grassy stage hosts a comedy show,
As fireflies twinkle, putting on a glow.

Grown-ups in suspense, as they trip on their feet,
Chasing a breeze that's playful and sweet.
The whispers of leaves, they giggle and sway,
In unity with laughter, they join in the play.

Pinecones drop lightly, like comical stars,
While squirrels debate how to mend their old cars.
With each silly twist, the forest breaks free,
A symphony of chaos, just wait, you'll see!

So, under this canopy, fun twirls around,
Where jokes take root, in the soft, fertile ground.
Embrace the absurd, let your spirits convene,
In the lullaby sung by the lasting green.

www.ingramcontent.com/pod-product-compliance
Lightning Source LLC
Chambersburg PA
CBHW070334120526
44590CB00017B/2880